Love with Vengeance
By
Luke Austin Daugherty

Copyright © 2005 Luke Austin Daugherty

Pilgrim's Journey Publishing

All rights reserved.

Cover design: Luke Austin Daugherty

Back cover photo: Lydia Daugherty

ISBN-10: 0692451145
ISBN-13: 978-0692451144

For Angela.

CONTENTS

1	Love with Vengeance	Pg 3
2	Come Near to Me My Love	Pg 4
3	Splash, Boom, Rhyme, Shh	Pg 5
4	Love #1	Pg 6
5	Love #2	Pg 7
6	Love #3	Pg 8
7	Love #4	Pg 9
8	Beautiful Sleeper	Pg 10
9	Essential	Pg 11
10	No Water in Venice	Pg 12
11	My Love	Pg 13
12	In the Shadow of Vesuvius	Pg 14
13	Lover… Make Haste	Pg 16
14	My Wife has a Gentle Heart	Pg 17
15	Love is Everest	Pg 18
16	She Wanted to Snuggle	Pg 19
17	Oh Sweet Love and the Glory of Making It	Pg 20
18	Love's Embrace	Pg 21
19	I Love You	Pg 22
20	The Chronicles of Simon the Lover	Pg 23

TO THE READER,

Once you have truly and selflessly loved another person, you will never be the same. Until you have, you will never know how "not-the-same" you have the potential to be. Love well and allow yourself be loved.

-Luke

LOVE WITH VENGEANCE

Lovers
Love with vengeance
Love as to war against
Your own frailty
Love as to seek revenge
Upon former occasions
When your love was not love
But a whim
And your passion
An impotent gesture
Subdue its territory
Overrun its defenseless borders
As it was love's manifest destiny
Be as a merciless conqueror
Treading his foes underfoot
Who at the end of his triumph
Holds his wearied sword high
Dripping with the blood
Of the vanquished
And gives an approving nod
To his fellow warriors
As if to say
Though in the heat of the battle
We have suffered loss
On this day of vengeance
Love has prevailed

COME NEAR TO ME MY LOVE

Come near to me my love
     And kiss me now
     With lips not closed
Come near to me my love
     And let us be one
     As we are one
Come near to me my love
     And let love have its way
     As it must
Come near to me my love
     And let our hearts be healed
     For they are torn with longing
Come near to me my love

SPLASH, BOOM, RHYME, SHH

Splash, splash
The thought of you
Drops constantly
Into the still waters
Of my being
Sending ripples
Into every corner
Of my existence

Boom, boom
Your rhythm
Eternally reverberates
Within the chambers
Of my heart
Making waves
Crash on the boundaries
Of my ocean

Rhyme, rhyme
Your poem
Writes always
On the pages
Of my thoughts
Inspiring wonder
In every realm
Of my mind

Shh, Shh
Your still voice
Forever hushing
The noisy unsurety
Of my soul
Forever silencing
Every question
Of my wondering

LOVE #1

It is temporal
It is eternal
Its fire consumes
Its ice chills
It is within
It is without
It is certain
It is unsure
It makes sense
It confounds
It shelters
It exposes
It shows itself able
It proves us incapable
It is life
It is death
It is love

LOVE #2

Tear my heart out
Please quickly
Hold it within my gaze
So that before I perish
I may view the chambers
Wherein you have dwelled
So forcefully
So flagrantly
So fully

LOVE #3

Love…
Flee from me
Flee!
For I am not worthy
Of your grace
Will you not heed
Though I increase my petition?
Flee!
Flee!
Flee!

Love…
If you will not depart
Then I must endure shame
For I am not worthy
Of your grace

LOVE #4

Love…
Be love
To me now

You are the sun and the moon
The solemn stars
Of a night sky

You are my victories
And my defeats

You are the
Bridges I have burned
Just to glory
In the rebuilding

Love…
Be love
To me now

BEAUTIFUL SLEEPER

Her beautiful form lie motionless
Still content with her slumber
She knows not that I observe with delight
My beautiful sleeper
The morning sun
Having not yet conquered the horizon
Glows in our bedroom
Its full strength censored
By our cotton drapes

Her hair
Brushed by the night
Obscures her sacred face
Her pink lips
Her perfect chin

Should I feel guilty
Stealing these moments
Like a cat burglar
Stealing precious jewels

No
I will plunder to my fill
As a thief with no conscience
For these are love's perfect moments
Not forced or coerced
The rare moments
When love just is

ESSENTIAL

She is a flower unaware of her blossom
So beautiful in her innocent unknowing
She is a promise preceded by hope
I am overcome with her
My eyes are nourished by her
My heart is starving
And overfull at the same time
Her presence is water and breath
She is essential

NO WATER IN VENICE

No water in Venice
How tragic the lover's fate
When a legion of saddened gondolas
Lay run aground
Tide has forsaken
The fair city
A solar system's syzygy
Casts canals to shallow depths

No gondolas to steer
Sporting couples through scenes of romance
While passion burns within
And twain stare into the other's eyes
As beholding doves flying

Is the cry of a lover's heart heard?

The question resounds
From our loins

Then from our stricken breast
The answer replies…

We shall revolt
Against the sun
And against the moon
We will move them
By the force of passion
Yes love will be the undoing
Of no water in Venice

MY LOVE

My heart is your prisoner
I am love's captive
Content in my bondage
Freedom is my enemy
I fear liberation
Our hearts are one heart
Love is our breath
Our survival

We complete each other

You laughingly flee from me
I chase you
And catch you
And desire you to flee again
So I could again pursue

As a rose petal drifting in a tempest
You bring beauty to chaos
You are the mystery and its answer
You are my love

IN THE SHADOW OF VESUVIUS

There is a people who dwell
In the shadow of Vesuvius
Who, though they live in constant danger
Savor the days and years
Spent in the volcano's hazard

They boldly proclaim
"These are our vineyards
And our homes for generations
In this place we eat our meat
And drink our wine with merry hearts
When the worst someday comes
We would be lost in its fury
Rather than forsake our heritage
For we are the people of Vesuvius"

So it is for we who choose to dwell
Under the mountain of true love
Our days are spent
In the veil of its wondrous shadow
We eat love's meat
And drink love's wine
With merry hearts

But we know
That those who choose to love
Choose ultimately to suffer
And when the worst comes
We would rather
Be lost in its fury
Than to have never known its grace

We are counted as fools
By the less courageous
Choosing the safety
Found far from the mountain's splendor
Who wince with pity

When they see us fall
Not realizing that they will fall also
For it is our common destiny

But we know it is more glorious
To fall in the presence of love
Than in its absence
It is this reason
We are as brethren
To those who dwell
In the shadow of Vesuvius

LOVER… MAKE HASTE

Lover…
Make haste
That we might meet
Quickly
And nourish each other's soul

Be not restrained
For our love
Is holy
And complete

Let our kisses
Be guided wisely
To neck and mouth
Let expectation
Tie knots in our stomachs
So that passion
May untie them

Let our love be such
That to label it "romance"
Would be cheap
And unjust

Lover…
Make haste

MY WIFE HAS A GENTLE HEART

My wife has a gentle heart
The flesh of it
Is soft
As the petal of a spring rose
It is tender
As the skin of a ripe pear
Its thoughts
Are innocent
Its motives
Are without guile
It has gravity
By which I am attracted
My wife has a gentle heart

LOVE IS EVEREST

Love's worth
Is found

In its difficulty

Love is precious
Because love is rare

We risk death
In our ascension of it

Because to stand
On its peak
With our chest straining
For breath
In the thinness
Of the high air

Is glorious

Love is Everest

SHE WANTED TO SNUGGLE

She wanted to snuggle
Early this morning

After two slaps
Of the snooze button
I attempted to rise
But her love restrained me
Her gentle arm
Around my abdomen
Her breath
Against my neck
Her naked feet
Teasing mine
A kiss
On my cheek

And with these
She did conquer my will
As I submitted to hers
And sank into her love

As a gratefully wounded ship
Into the ocean

OH SWEET LOVE AND THE GLORY OF MAKING IT

Oh sweet love
And the glory of making it
Be known to me
Once again

You, as the Proverb suggests
Are a thing
Too wonderful for me
The way of a man with a maid
This night
Proverb
Prove yourself again
In love
And its expression
Of twain becoming one
Let passion
As a hot
Burning coal
Be placed within my breast
That the pure water
Of my lover's heart
May do its worst
To be the extinguishing

Oh sweet love
And the glory of making it

LOVE'S EMBRACE

When love's embrace comes
It brings with itself
A pair of wings

Wings that carry you through midnight storms
When the rain is hard
And lightning flashes all around

Wings that fly high on cool spring breezes
Above all the newness
And the fruit of nature's rebirth

Wings that glide over the process of time
As the years unfold
And the future becomes the past

Wings that can soar on joy or sorrow
For their contrasts
Become the texture of our lives
As love weaves
From the thread of life's moments
A tapestry without seams

And with its embrace
Comes a pair of wings

I LOVE YOU

To the one who stole my heart with a hug
   I love you
To the answer to my prayer
   I love you
To the one my heart longs for
   I love you
To the one who looked so beautiful in her wedding dress
   I love you
To the one who sees beyond my faults
   I love you
To the mother of my children
   I love you
To the one I will grow old with
   I love you
To the one who meant, "Till death do we part."
   I love you
And to the better part of me
   I love you

THE CHRONICLES OF SIMON THE LOVER

Chapter One: A Man Peculiar
Chapter Two: The Heart of Simon
Chapter Three: The Revelation
         Of St. Simon
Chapter Four: A Poet's Encounter
Chapter Five: Chronicle #1
Chapter Six: Curiosity
Chapter Seven: Chronicle #2
Chapter Eight: Muriel's Heart
Chapter Nine: Chronicle #3
Chapter Ten: Fallen Angel
Chapter Eleven: Chronicle #4
Chapter Twelve: Muriel's Redemption

Chapter One: A Man Peculiar

Every small town has a man who is shunned
A man who is peculiar in one way or another
Usually seen walking here or there
Sometimes stopping at the cafe for coffee
Sitting in the safety of the back-corner booth
Always alone

A man who is never afforded
The congenial small talk
And courteous nods
Offered to one another
By the regular citizens

Simon was such a man

He had suffered a bout of polio as a child
Scarcely surviving the episode
Being left a bit hunched over
With his spine and one leg permanently crooked

In 1956
Simon was a man in his late twenties
He was always disheveled in appearance
Often seen shuffling down the sidewalk
While catching the disapproving glances
Of the regular townsfolk
Like an unwelcome leper with
Worn clothes
Unkempt hair
And a lonely soul

His parents having both passed on
He lived with an aunt on his father's side
Who was kind enough to give him room and board
Though he could pay no regular rent
As he was only able to find odd and infrequent jobs
Because who wants a cripple for their hired man

(Strange how a town with so many churches
can be so wanting in the area of practical
Christianity)

Chapter Two: The Heart of Simon

In spite of his lack of human friends
Simon was not completely forsaken
For he found the companionship offered by books
To be quite agreeable
His best pals were the Scriptures, Moby Dick
And a collection of love poems
Penned by the great writers of verse

Oh,
And by the way
Simon was in love

Her name was Muriel
She was an angel in his eyes

Every time he saw her in town
His heart felt as though it was being crushed
By the mighty hand of God

But he would only look quickly
For he was the town's peculiar one
And though he could bear the judgmental stares
Of everyone who passed him by

To risk catching such a glance from Muriel
Would be as death to him
So rather than chance such a fate
He withheld his eyes from ever meeting hers

For several years
Simon had lived in that sad state
A man whose chest burned with the heat
Of true love's passion
Yet he felt imprisoned
Unable to express his deepest emotions
To the object of his desire
The sweet Muriel

But one day
Everything changed…

Chapter Three: The Revelation of St. Simon

Simon was deep in his daily Bible study
Making his devotion in the book of Proverbs
One of his favorite portions of Scripture
When he came across one fateful verse
Proverbs 27:5
"Open rebuke is better than secret love"

It was as though a fog was lifted
From his lonesome soul
As his God's words gave the charge

And a spark of liberating revelation
Was ignited

Though his mind had been quickened
He yet reasoned within himself
"How can a man such as I
Shunned and despised of all
Express to the beautiful rose, Muriel
The truest feelings of my heart?"

He was frustrated
By the apparent contradiction
Why would God provoke him to action
While offering no course
To accomplish the task

As the battle raged
In his smitten heart
He found the answer
In the notion of a faithful friend
At the moment he looked upon the book of prose
That had also been his meditation many lonely hours

He would pour out his heart in verse
Page and pen would play the music
Of his love song
And Muriel would finally know
That he loved her

But he could not just walk right up to her
At the corner of Main and Jefferson
And hand her the love letter in an envelope

For he was the town's peculiar one
Such an action would surely be disastrous

Simon decided on a less direct course
He would offer his love poems for publication
In the community contribution section

Of the local newspaper
The Town Chronicle

Chapter Four: A Poet's Encounter

The next day
Simon sat in his usual
Back-corner booth at the diner
Feeling isolated and safe
From the judgment of the normal townsfolk
Hoping Muriel
Who worked as a teller at the bank across the street
Would follow her usual routine
And come to the diner for lunch

A few minutes later
When Muriel walked in
It was to Simon
As the gates of Heaven opening
With celestial light shining upon her face
And her dark brown hair

Simon's ballpoint pen felt like the ready
Ink-dipped quill of a prophet
While the words flowed freely onto the lined page of
His new dime store notebook
As did those on Solomon's scroll
When he wrote his sacred Song

Simon penned the words purposefully
And with great thought and reflection
As though he was whispering the sonnet
In Muriel's ear
His head just over her cashmere covered shoulder

When Simon's confession was finished
He carefully tore out the page
Folded it neatly, with even creases

Until it was one third its original size
Just the perfect fit for a fresh, white envelope

Once the envelope was licked, sealed, and stamped
Simon wrote the "To" address on the front
But added no "From"
Then mailed it to *The Town Chronicle*

Though the newspaper's office
Was only two blocks away
Simon wished for the time being
To remain anonymous
And could not risk being noticed
Dropping the letter off
For he was the town's peculiar one

Simon chose rather
To drop it into the large, metal mailbox
On the corner of the sidewalk
Feeling gravity pull it out of his fingers
Before he allowed the heavy, tilt-out mail slot door
To swing back into place

Simon
Knowing what he had done
Could not be undone
He whispered to himself
"It is finished"

Upon the poem's publishing
In *The Town Chronicle*
Several days later
It could be said that there was no small stir
Among the populace of the small town
For Simon was plain
With the notions of his heart

His anonymous, yet public confession
Read in this fashion…

Chapter Five: Chronicle #1

"Muriel
You are the sweetest fragrance
Of the fairest May flower

My heart is stricken
In every moment
Of your absence

Your beauty draws my soul
In the night watches
As the moon's gravity
Upon the ocean tide

If I believed but for a moment
That there was not a place
For our love
I would beg not to love you

Will my confession
Find a kind answer?
Will you forgive my secrets?
Will your sacrifice
Be my love's salvation?
Does your heart hear
My whispered prayer?

Oh Muriel
Suffer love's fool to speak!"

Chapter Six: Curiosity

All wondered and asked amongst themselves
"Who is the author of this outpouring?
These are not the words of a simple man
Or of a plain, small town fellow.
The author of this poem is surely
One to be esteemed for his love and words"

What of Muriel?
Let's just say her smile was a bit
Wider than usual that day
And her heart beat harder
Than it ever had
Energized by such curiosity alive within her

And Simon?
He saw her smiling
And it was the best day of his life
Though many men have provoked
One thousand smiles from the one they love
For Simon
This was the first

Once again they had lunch together
From across the room
Muriel smiled and chatted
With her girlfriends from the bank
And Simon spoke silently with his pen
But with a greater sense of freedom
Than before

Off went another letter
To *The Town Chronicle*
It was in the paper only two days later
And the expectation of the town
(And of Muriel)
Was not disappointed

Chapter 7: Chronicle #2

"Oh, Muriel
Be my song once more!
From the marrow of my bones
I long for your response
Will I be received?
Or will you reckon my love grotesque?
I cannot much longer bear
But to know love's fate

My most pure dove
Desire of a heart not defiled
Do you believe my motives are true?
My thoughts toward you are holy

From antiquity to this present age
None as you was ever found
Your smile is as
The birth of dawn
From the eastward horizon
To have but the hope of you
Is better than Solomon's riches
Yet my soul desires more than hope

Muriel
Will your heart find place for my love?"

Chapter Eight: Muriel's Heart

As Muriel read the poem
She wept
And that moment brought a first for her
She believed for the first time
That true love was real
And her heart began to yearn
To know who her lover was

As she made her way through the day
Every moment felt like a lifetime
Each man she passed
Brought the same question
"Is this my love?"

With Simon's words
The door to Muriel's heart
Had been unlocked

That day when Simon saw her
He saw a woman in love
But she didn't know who with
One moment she giggled to herself
The next she was almost in tears

Simon was resolved…

He would be revealed
To his love
And it would be for Muriel
To slay him or bring him to life

When he left the diner after lunch
He walked straight to the front desk of *The Town Chronicle*
And personally delivered the letter

The whole walk home
And the rest of the day
Simon did nothing
But hope against hope

And as he slept
He saw Muriel in his dreams

The following day's paper
Had his poem on the front page

Chapter Nine: Chronicle #3

"Beloved Muriel
You are my only desire
I am your captive
Do with me as you wish
I will be revealed to you
Shroud not your eyes
But look full on
I wish not to be a spectacle
But a welcome revelation
Muriel my blessed flower

My stomach is in knots
Yet I will not be ruled by fear
For I believe in love
And I trust my lover's heart
Be my answered prayer
My Muriel
My love
I am Simon"

Chapter Ten: Fallen Angel

And with that
Time stopped in the small community
While everyone who had bought a paper
Caught their breath
(And believe me,
that day everyone bought a paper)

On Simon's way into town
Each passing car moved in slow motion
And every pedestrian's glance
Was not a look of disgust
But of amazed confusion

Simon?

The town's peculiar one?
Can a crooked, shuffling
Familiar stranger
Be the author of inspired words
And the true love
Of the fair Muriel?

Could he be the one
Who had cut his heart open
As with a knife
Before us all?

That day at the diner
Simon was not the ghost
Haunting the back-corner table
But the focus of everyone's attention
And topic of their whispered conversation

As twelve o'clock drew nearer
Simon's anticipation increased
And when the door opened
His heart almost ceased to beat
When for the first time
He allowed his eyes to meet Muriel's

Between each blink
Eternity passed
Muriel felt Simon's love
She felt peace
She felt whole

Then, as when Peter took his eyes off of the Lord and
Sunk into the sea
With faith faltering
Muriel looked upon the faces of the townsfolk
Felt their judgment
And with her faith in love shaken
She ran back out the door

As she hurried down the sidewalk
She wept with disappointment
Not in her lover
But in herself
Her detached, offended spirit
Viewed her body from above
As God, beholding a fallen angel

Simon sat at his formica covered
Back-corner table
And wrote one last poem for *The Town Chronicle*

Chapter Eleven: Chronicle #4

"Is now my true destiny revealed
A lover never to be loved?
Beloved Muriel
I cannot be angry with you
I am angry with my crooked spine
Damn my crooked leg!
They have been love's stumbling block
Muriel, our hearts are pure

But our circumstance is corrupt
And will not suffer
Love's flower to blossom
My love, I will leave this small town
I refuse any longer to be suffocated
By its hypocritical judgment

I will go to the city
Where a peculiar man
May better blend in
As a large crowd
Provides a capable camouflage
For a lonely soul

I take no suitcase

A lover's heart
Is the only baggage I carry
I am sorry that
I was not found pleasing
To you
My love
Muriel
Goodbye"

Chapter Twelve: Muriel's Redemption

At the delivery of the morning paper
Muriel's heart broke
How could she have passed judgment
On true love?
How could she have fallen prey
To her own weakness?
To her own shameful pride?
She knew her course of action…

The following day
Another letter was published
In *The Town Chronicle*
But from a different author

"To the town where I was born
And the town where I have spent my life
We beheld true love smile
And we frowned back in disapproval
We heard love's confession

As priests with deaf ears
We have all sinned in judgment
I must tell you goodbye
I go to the city
To find my love
With sweet regret,
Muriel"

For more information on Luke Austin Daugherty:

Official Sites-

lukeaustindaugherty.com

loveisthemiddle.com

Official Blog-
lukeaustindaugherty.wordpress.com

Contact:

lukeaustindaugherty@gmail.com

www.ingramcontent.com/pod-product-compliance
Lightning Source LLC
Chambersburg PA
CBHW031507040426
42444CB00007B/1237